EXPERIMENT WITH
WATER

Written by Bryan Murphy

Science Consultant: Dr. Christine Sutton
Nuclear Physics Department, University of Oxford

Education Consultant: Ruth Bessant

TWO CAN

LONDON ■ PRINCETON

www.two-canpublishing.com

Published by Two-Can Publishing,
43-45 Dorset Street, London W1U 7NA

© 2002, 1991 Two-Can Publishing
Text © Bryan Murphy, 1991

For information on Two-Can books and multimedia,
call (0)20 7224 2440, fax (0)20 7224 7005, or visit our website at
http://www.two-canpublishing.com

Author: Bryan Murphy
Illustrator: Sally Kindberg
Designer: Linda Blakemore
Science Consultant: Dr. Christine Sutton
Education Consultant: Ruth Bessant

'Two-Can' is a trademark of Two-Can Publishing.
Two-Can Publishing is a division of Zenith Entertainment Ltd,
43-45 Dorset Street, London W1U 7NA

PB ISBN 1-84301-034-8

PB 1 2 3 4 5 6 7 8 9 10 04 03 02

All photographs are copyright © Fiona Pragoff, except for the following: cover, Ray Moller;
pp. 4, 5 (bottom right), 10, 18, 19 (top), 23 (bottom), ZEFA Picture Library (UK) Ltd.;
pp. 5 (top centre, top right, bottom left), 23 (top), Science Photo Library;
p. 8, Oxford Scientific Films; pp. 8 (inset), 9 (centre), Frank Lane Picture Agency Ltd.;
pp. 9 (top and bottom) 26, 27 (centre), Ardea; pp. 12, 21, 27 (top), Bruce Coleman Ltd.

Printed in Hong Kong by Wing King Tong

CONTENTS

All words marked in **bold** can be found in the glossary

WATER ALL AROUND US

Water, water, water. Wherever we look there is usually something to do with water. Have you ever stopped and thought about it? Here are some fascinating water facts.

◀ There are about 1,500 million million cubic metres of water on the Earth, but none on the Moon.

▶ Water can be **boiled** into **steam** or frozen into **ice**.

▼ When things burn, they give off steam.

▼ Scientists call water H_2O! One litre of water weighs exactly one kilogram.

THE WATER CYCLE

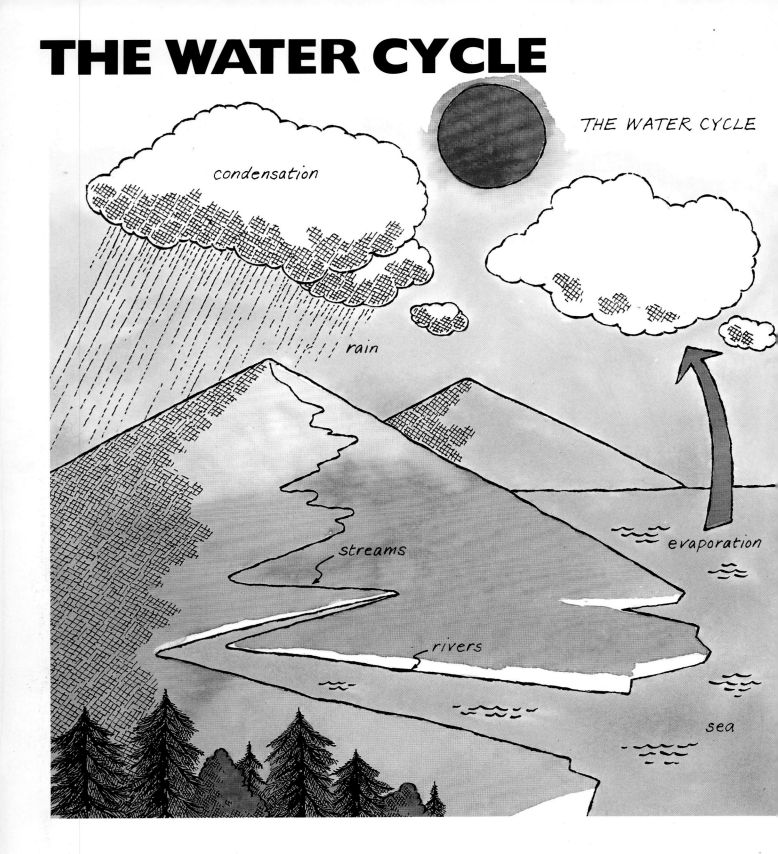

condensation

THE WATER CYCLE

rain

streams

rivers

evaporation

sea

There is a lot of water on the Earth. Most of it is in the huge seas and **oceans**. Some of it is in **lakes** and **rivers**, and some of it is high above us in the **clouds**. Have you noticed something about water? It is hardly ever still. **Energy** from the Sun sends the water from the sea on a long journey, called the **water cycle**.

◀ You can create the whole of the water cycle in your home.

Pour a little water on to a plate. Leave it on a windowsill or shelf overnight. In the morning, you may be able to see that the level has gone down a little. Where do you think the water has gone? It has turned from liquid water into water **vapour**. This vapour has been taken into the air. Water from the sea is taken into the air by the wind. What happens next?

▼ On a cold day the warm water vapour in a bathroom **condenses** on the mirror, and drops of water dribble down the cold glass like rain.

WATER AND THE WEATHER

All over the world the weather is different. Water plays an important part in the weather, and it can appear in many forms.

► Inside a cloud there are lots of tiny water droplets. If they bump into each other they join together and get larger. When they are big enough, the droplets fall out of the cloud as rain.

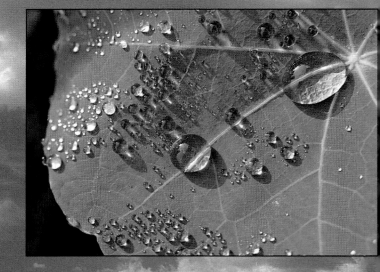

▶ If the air near the ground has a lot of water vapour in it and is cooled, the water vapour condenses and forms a ground level cloud. This is called **fog**.

◀ Sometimes it is very cold in a cloud, less than 0° centigrade. At this temperature the water droplets in a cloud freeze together to form tiny crystals of ice. The crystals stick together and when the air below the cloud is also cold, the ice falls as **snow**.

◀ The air in a cloud is always moving. If an ice crystal is swept through a large cloud by rising winds, it can grow into a larger ball of ice. This is called **hail**. A hailstone the size of a melon fell on a town called Coffeyville in Kansas, USA on 3 September 1970.

WATER PRESSURE

Have you ever tried to touch the bottom of a swimming pool? Sometimes when you try, you can feel the water pressing on your ears. This is because the water has a **pressure** which is pushing on your eardrums. As you go deeper, the pressure gets greater and your ears may hurt.

Try holding your head at different angles. You can still feel the pressure of the water. Pressure pushes in all directions. If you want to try this at home or at your swimming pool make sure that an adult or lifeguard is nearby.

▼ Seals always close up their nostrils and ear-holes when they dive deeply.

Ask an adult to help you make three holes in the sides of a plastic bottle, using the sharp point of some scissors. Get a friend to help you with the next bit, because you need three hands.

With your friend cover up the holes with your fingers and fill the bottle with water. Quickly take your fingers away. The water will spurt from the holes. Which hole has the biggest jet of water? Why do you think this is?

MAKING A SUBMARINE

Submarines are special boats that can go under water. They have to be strong so that the great pressure deep under the ocean does not crush them.

UNDERSEAS DEVELOP

It is easy to make a submarine that dives and surfaces just like the real thing. You can amaze your friends by making it go up and down without touching it – just like magic!

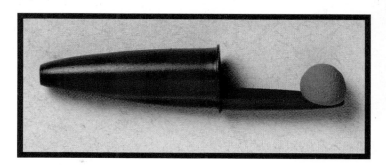

▲ All you need is the top of a pen, some modelling clay, and a plastic bottle with a lid. Put a small blob of the clay on the end of a long, thin pen top.

▼ Carefully put the top in a bottle full of water and screw the bottle lid on tightly. The pen top will float near the surface of the water.

Now for the clever bit. Ask your friends if they want the pen top to float or **sink.** You can control it by squeezing the sides of the bottle. Try it, it really works!

WEIGHT AND VOLUME

About 2,000 years ago the King of Syracuse in Greece bought a golden crown. He was told that the crown was made of solid gold, but he wanted to make sure. The King asked a very clever man called Archimedes to check how much pure gold his crown was made of, without harming it.

Archimedes suddenly realised how he could check the crown when he was getting into the bath. He was so excited that he ran down the street. Unfortunately he forgot to get dressed!

Archimedes filled a basin with water. He put the king's crown in the basin and caught the water that spilled out, so that he could weigh it. He also weighed the crown, to find out how many times heavier it was than water. Then he weighed a piece of pure gold, to find out how many times heavier than water pure gold is. By weighing how much water spilled out when the crown was put in the basin, he could tell if the crown was pure gold.

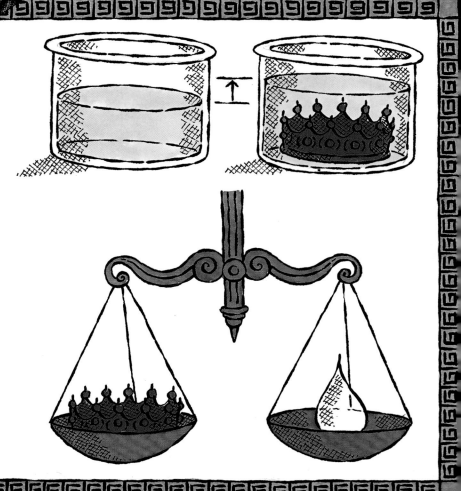

◀ Next time you have a bath, see what happens to the level of the water. Before you climb in, mark the top level of the water with a wax crayon. Now get into the bath and mark the new level. Look at the difference in height between the two marks. An object will push up the level of water by the amount of space it takes up, or its **volume**. You have just measured the volume of your body!

Do not forget to wipe off the wax marks after the experiment.

Try this experiment to measure the volume of something a lot cheaper than a golden crown, such as a stone! Put exactly 500 ml of water into a measuring jug. Carefully put a stone into the jug and measure the new level of the water.

▶ When Toni did this the water level rose from 500 ml to 600 ml. The stone took the place of 100 ml of water and pushed the level up.

One millilitre is the same amount as one cubic centimetre. What do you think the volume of Toni's stone was?

FLOATING AND SINKING

Have you ever noticed that some things float and some things sink? Make a collection of things from around the house and guess which ones will float and which ones will sink.

▲ Then fill a clear glass or plastic tank or bucket with water. Put the things in the water. Were you surprised? Did you think that the heavy things would sink and the light ones float?

Next time you go to a swimming pool try lifting a friend in the water. You will find your friend is much heavier to lift on land.

◀ Try **submerging** something that floats. You have to push to make it go under the surface of the water. How long does it take to rise up to the surface again?

▼ Fill a balloon or see-through polythene bag with water. Tell a friend that you can make it weigh nothing! Push the balloon under the water. It does not float or sink because it contains water, and so weighs the same as the water around it.

LOOKING AT BOATS

There are many different types of boat. Their shape and size depend on what job they do. See if you can design and make two different types of boat out of modelling clay.

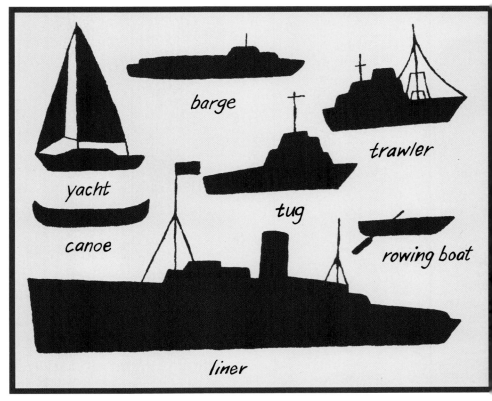

yacht

barge

trawler

tug

canoe

rowing boat

liner

▶An **oil tanker** is a huge boat that carries crude oil. It has to hold a lot of oil and float in very shallow water in harbours. Look at this picture of an oil tanker. What do you notice about its shape? Is it short, long, thin or wide?

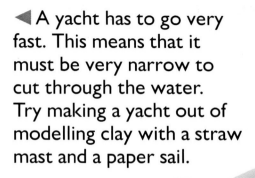

◀ A yacht has to go very fast. This means that it must be very narrow to cut through the water. Try making a yacht out of modelling clay with a straw mast and a paper sail.

▼ Float your boat in the bath and blow on the sail. How can you make it go faster? See what happens if you change the shape of the sail or make the boat narrower.

SURFACE TENSION

There is something very peculiar that happens to the surface of water. You have to get very close and look very carefully to see it.

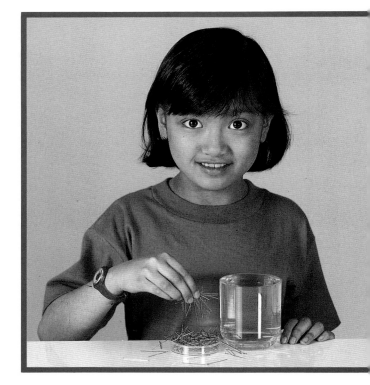

▶ Ask a friend a simple question. How many pins at a time can she put in a glass full to the brim with water, without any water spilling over? You'd think the answer is none. Try it! Now ask her to put the pins in one at a time. How many can she fit in the glass: 5, 10, 20, 40? Look closely at the surface of the water. Instead of pouring out, the water seems to be held in by an invisible skin. This is called **surface tension**.

▶ You might be surprised to find out how strong the skin on the surface of water is. Do you think it can support a pin even though the pin is made of heavy metal?
Carefully float a small piece of kitchen paper on water. Quickly drop a pin on it and watch what happens when the paper sinks. The pin is left on the water's surface. If you look very closely, you should be able to see where the surface is holding it up.
Pins are very sharp so be careful how you handle them.

Some water insects, called water
boatmen, can walk on water without
getting their feet wet. They can also
walk upside-down, suspended from the
water's surface.

BUBBLES

When washing-up liquid is added to water, it makes the skin at the surface more stretchy. This means that you can make **bubbles**!

▲ Gently mix about one cup of washing-up liquid with five cups of warm water in a mixing bowl. To make even better bubbles add about one teaspoon of a secret ingredient, glycerine. If the mixture doesn't work at once, try mixing different amounts of the ingredients.

▲ You can have great fun with your bubble mixture. Ask an adult to help you make a bubble pipe by cutting four slits in the end of a straw. Fold out the flaps. They support the bubble as it gets bigger. Scoop up some of the bubble mixture into a tea-cup. Dip the bubble pipe briefly into the surface of the liquid and then blow gently.

If it is a cold day, try blowing your bubbles outside. When you fill the bubbles with your breath, you are filling them with warm air.

Which way do the bubbles go, up or down? Why do you think this is? Warm air rises and helps the bubble go up in the cold air.

◀ Look closely at a bubble. Can you see beautiful colours in it? Where have you seen colours like this before?

▼ The colours on the surface of a bubble are all the colours of the rainbow.

SEPARATING COLOURS

How black is black ink? Is it really made from a mixture of colours? This experiment shows you how to use water to find out. All you need is some white blotting paper, black ink, a glass, a pair of scissors and, of course, some water.

►Cut a circle out of the blotting paper a bit larger than the top of the glass. Put a small blot of ink in the centre. Next, make two cuts in the blotting paper and fold the middle strip down. Carefully place the blotting paper over the top of the glass with the thin strip in the water. Watch closely and you won't believe your eyes!

As the water slowly soaks up into the blotting paper, it separates the ink into colours. This is called **chromatography**, which means "colour drawing". Try it with different coloured inks or food colouring to see what colours they are made of.

24

ALL-PURPOSE WATER

Water is very useful. We use it for all sorts of things around the house: washing, drinking, watering plants. Waste water from our households is cleaned at a sewage farm before finally flowing out to sea. How many other uses of water can you think of?

To be sure of a good water supply to people's houses all year round, **dams** can be built across rivers to make artificial lakes called **reservoirs**. In wet weather the reservoirs fill up and store water which can be used later. In countries all over the world, reservoirs are also used to store water for **irrigation**. Where there is little rain local farmers can channel this water over their fields to feed their crops.

Water is a source of power. Try holding your thumb over the end of a hose-pipe with water flowing into it. If you take your thumb away, the water will gush out.

◀ Watermills use the **force** of falling water. The rushing water of a stream pours along a special channel and on to the blades of a huge water wheel at the side of a mill. As the wheel turns, machinery inside the mill grinds huge stones together. In the past these mills were used to crush corn into flour.

◀ Nowadays the force of falling water is used to provide **electricity** for whole cities. Some dams store water in reservoirs high up in the mountains. Big pipes bring the water gushing downhill to **hydro-electric power stations**. There, the water pushes against the blades of a **turbine** – rather like a water wheel. As the turbine spins quickly, it works the generator and makes the electricity.

MAKE YOUR OWN WATER WHEEL

Here is an experiment to get power from moving water. You will need some card, an old cotton reel, a straw and some double-sided sticky tape.

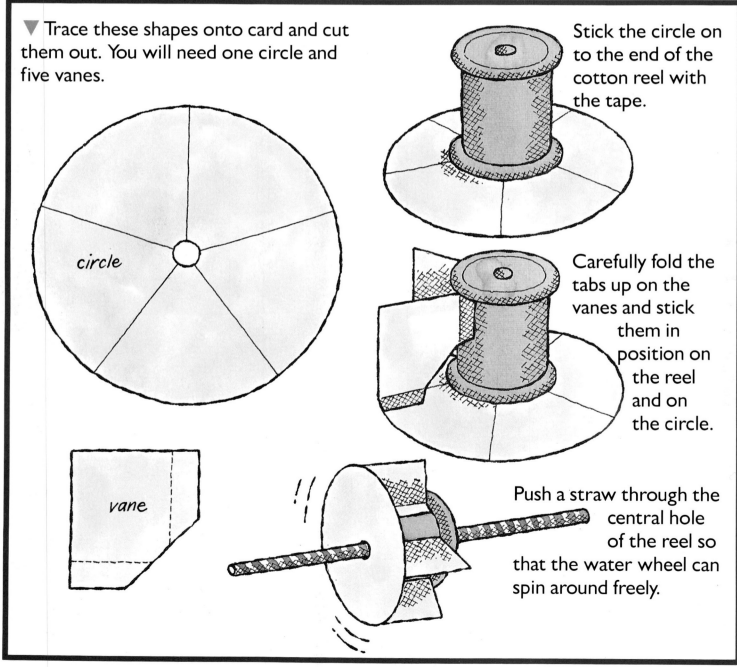

▼ Trace these shapes onto card and cut them out. You will need one circle and five vanes.

circle

vane

Stick the circle on to the end of the cotton reel with the tape.

Carefully fold the tabs up on the vanes and stick them in position on the reel and on the circle.

Push a straw through the central hole of the reel so that the water wheel can spin around freely.

 Try spinning the wheel in the kitchen sink under running water from the tap. Where does it spin fastest? When it is near the tap's spout or further down the stream of water? Why do you think this is? Where is the water moving fastest?

Draw some patterns on the wheel and watch it spin round.

29

GLOSSARY

Boiling turns a liquid into a gas by heating.

Bubbles are gas (like air) trapped in a liquid casing.

Clouds are formed when water droplets or ice crystals are held in the air.

Condensation turns a gas or vapour into a liquid by cooling.

Dam is a man-made blockage or wall holding back water.

Electricity is a type of energy used to make bulbs light up, turn motors, etc.

Energy is needed by all things to be active.

Floating is resting on the surface of water.

Fog is made when clouds are near the ground.

Hail is small lumps of ice falling to the ground.

Hydro-electric power station is where electricity is made by falling water pushed through turbines.

Ice is frozen water.

Lake is a large natural body of water.

Ocean is a huge body of salt water.

Oil tanker is a big boat used to carry oil.

Pressure is the weight of something on an area.

Rain is water droplets falling to the ground.

Reservoir is a man-made lake behind a dam.

River is water flowing over land and carving a channel for itself.

Sinking is falling in a liquid.

Snow is frozen water falling to the ground as crystals.

Steam is small water droplets in the air.

Submarine is a boat that can go underwater.

Submerge is to push underwater.

Surface tension is the invisible "skin" on the surface of water.

Turbine is a spinning motor, pushed around by moving water or steam.

Volume is the space that something takes up.

Water cycle is the movement of water from the seas and oceans to the clouds, then to rain and rivers and back again to the seas.

Water vapour is water in the atmosphere or air.

Weight is the force with which something pushes downwards.

Yacht is a sailing boat built for cruising or racing.

INDEX

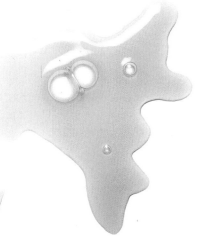

For more information about TWO-CAN books, write to TWO-CAN Publishing, 346 Old Street, London, EC1V 9NQ.